What Should I Be?

by F. Isabel Campoy
illustrated by Daniel Clifford

Harcourt

Orlando   Boston   Dallas   Chicago   San Diego

Visit The Learning Site!
www.harcourtschool.com

Mr. Moore, our teacher, likes to ask questions that make us think. Today he said, "I want you to think hard about a career you would like. Then I want you to find out about that career and write a report about it. Be ready to give a speech to the class."

We all started talking at once.
"I want to be a singer!" said Karen.
"I want to be an accountant like my Uncle Raul!" said David.
"One at a time!" said Mr. Moore, laughing. "Let's brainstorm some careers. I'll write them on the board. You might get some new ideas."
Mr. Moore wrote singer and accountant. "What else?" he asked.
Pilot! Architect! Musician! Baseball player! Veterinarian! Ice-cream store owner!
Mr. Moore wrote all our ideas on the board. I read the list of careers and thought hard.

3

What should I be? Maybe I should be an astronaut!

An astronaut has to know a lot about space. I know a lot about the planets. I know that there are rings around Saturn and a big, red spot on Jupiter. I know that Jupiter is the largest planet in our solar system.

I know that there is no gravity in space. People can float around because they are weightless.

An astronaut has to work well with the other astronauts on the space shuttle or space station. I am good at getting along with people. Astronauts have a lot of work to do. They might have to fix a satellite. They do experiments that could help people on Earth.

Maybe I should be an astronaut…

What should I be? Maybe I should be a chef!

A chef has to know a lot about cooking. I know how to make tacos and ice-cream sundaes. I know how much salt and pepper to add to some foods to make them taste better.

A chef has to work well with the other people in a restaurant kitchen. Everyone has a special job to do to make sure each meal is made well. I help Mami and Papi in the kitchen when they make dinner. My special job is making the salad.

A chef might be asked to invent new recipes. I have lots of ideas for new recipes. The food has to look as good as it tastes. I would arrange it on the plate to make it look beautiful.

Some chefs write their own cookbooks. I would like to write a cookbook. Maybe I could have my own cooking show on TV! I would show people how to follow my recipes.

Maybe I should be a chef…

What should I be? Maybe I should be a doctor!

My mother is a doctor, and she loves her job. A doctor has to know a lot about medicine. He or she cares about sick people and wants to help them get better. I like to help people feel better.

I would learn how to read X rays and fix broken bones. I would try to make children smile and not feel afraid.

A doctor has to know how to help people stay healthy. I know a lot about healthful foods. There is a poster in my classroom of the food pyramid. It shows how many servings of each kind of food to eat each day.

I would learn about the vitamins and minerals my patients need. I would tell them how important it is to exercise every day.

Maybe I should be a doctor…

What should I be? Maybe I should be a firefighter!

My father is a firefighter, and he loves his job. A firefighter has to be brave. He or she may have to rescue people from flames and smoke. Firefighters have to be ready to put out fires at all times of the day or night.

Firefighters have to learn to drive a fire truck quickly but carefully. When they get to the fire, they have to work together as a team to put the fire out. They have to be strong to carry fire hoses and other equipment. They may also have to carry people out of a burning building. I think I could be brave in an emergency.

Maybe I should be a firefighter…

What should I be? Maybe I should be a sound engineer!

A sound engineer must know a lot about music. He or she has to know what to do to make a song sound better.

I like music, and I know a lot about it. I would like to learn how to use the equipment in a sound studio. I would like to learn how to make songs sound great.

A sound engineer has to know a lot about musical instruments. I can play the piano, but I would have to learn about the guitar, drums, and bass. I would have to learn about the trumpet, saxophone, and violin, too.

A sound engineer has to know about many different kinds of music. I like every kind of music.

Maybe I should be a sound engineer…

What should I be? Maybe I should be a teacher!

A teacher must know a lot about many different subjects. He or she has to help all kinds of students. Mr. Moore is a very good teacher. He works hard in the classroom. He also takes work home with him. I guess teachers have homework, too!

If I were a teacher, I could help students learn.

I would know how to answer questions about English, Math, Social Studies, and Science.

I could tell students how to study for tests.

I would be fair when I graded their papers. I would tell them what they did well. I would also tell them what they needed to improve.

I like to learn, and I like to help other people.

Maybe I should be a teacher…

There are so many careers to choose from—I wish I could have them all!

I will write my report about being an astronaut, but I know I may change my mind.

What should I be? I don't know yet, but someday I will!